AI and THE JUSTICE SYSTEM

A STRONG CASE

EMMANUEL JOHN LUTWICK

Copyright 2024

The mother of my children is a lawyer. I always had an interest in the law. More importantly I am an AI enthusiast/expert, technology guru and researcher. I put this book together with heart, knowledge and for my two boys Timothy and Eric.

Whether your a lawyer, in the legal profession or a person with curiosity, this book is for everyone.

Enjoy and Learn

Emmanuel Lutwick, Author

Outline

I. Introduction
- Overview of Artificial Intelligence (AI)
- Relevance and integration of AI in various fields
- Purpose and scope of the story

II. The Evolution of AI
- Early developments in AI
- Key milestones in AI research
- Current state of AI technology

III. AI in the Legal System: An Overview
- Introduction to AI applications in law
- Examples of AI tools used in the legal system
- Benefits and challenges of AI in legal practice

IV. AI and Legal Research
- How AI enhances legal research
- Case studies of AI in legal research
- Future prospects of AI in legal research

V. AI in Predictive Analytics
- Introduction to predictive analytics in law

X. Case Studies of AI in the Legal System

- Detailed case studies

- Successes and failures

- Lessons learned

XI. The Future of AI and the Legal System

- Predictions and trends

- Potential challenges

- The evolving relationship between AI and law

XII. Conclusion

- Summary of key points

- The impact of AI on the legal system

- Final thoughts

I. Introduction

Artificial Intelligence (AI) has rapidly transformed various sectors of society, demonstrating its potential to revolutionize the way we live and work. With advancements in machine learning, neural networks, and natural language processing, AI has moved from the realm of science fiction to practical, everyday applications. From healthcare to finance, AI's ability to process large amounts of data, identify patterns, and make decisions has proven invaluable.

In recent years, the legal industry has begun to explore the potential of AI to streamline processes, enhance decision-making, and improve access to justice. As legal professionals grapple with increasing volumes of data and the need for more efficient solutions, AI offers tools that can significantly augment traditional practices. These tools range from legal research platforms powered by AI to predictive analytics that forecast case outcomes, and even automated contract analysis.

However, the integration of AI into the legal system also raises several important questions. How do we ensure that AI tools adhere to ethical standards and legal regulations? What are the implications of AI-driven decisions in a system that values human judgment and discretion? How can the legal profession balance the benefits of AI with the potential risks and challenges it presents?

This story delves into the multifaceted relationship between artificial intelligence and the legal system. We will explore the historical development of AI, its current applications in the legal field, and the potential future directions of this technology. Through detailed case studies, ethical discussions, and analysis of legal frameworks, we aim to provide a comprehensive understanding of how AI is reshaping the legal landscape.

By examining both the opportunities and challenges presented by AI, this story seeks to illuminate the path forward for legal professionals, policymakers, and technologists. The journey of AI in the legal system is one of innovation, adaptation, and continuous learning, reflecting the broader societal shifts towards a more technologically integrated future.

II. The Evolution of AI

The journey of artificial intelligence began long before the digital age, rooted in philosophical and mathematical inquiries about the nature of intelligence and the possibility of creating machines that could replicate human thought processes. Early conceptualizations of AI can be traced back to ancient myths and legends, where automatons and artificial beings were imagined by various cultures.

Early Developments in AI:
The formal study of AI as a scientific discipline began in the mid-20th century. Alan Turing, a British mathematician, is often credited with laying the groundwork for AI with his seminal 1950 paper, "Computing Machinery and Intelligence." In this paper, Turing introduced the idea of the "Turing Test," a criterion for determining whether a machine can exhibit intelligent behavior indistinguishable from that of a human.

The 1956 Dartmouth Conference is widely regarded as the birth of AI as an academic field. Organized by John McCarthy, Marvin Minsky, Nathaniel Rochester, and Claude Shannon, this conference brought together researchers interested in the possibility of creating machines that could simulate human intelligence. The term "artificial intelligence" was coined during this conference, marking the beginning of a new era in computing.

Key Milestones in AI Research:

The decades following the Dartmouth Conference saw significant advancements in AI research. In the 1960s and 1970s, early AI programs such as ELIZA, a natural language processing program, and SHRDLU, a program capable of understanding and manipulating objects in a virtual world, demonstrated the potential of AI in language understanding and problem-solving.

The 1980s and 1990s were characterized by the development of expert systems, which used rule-based approaches to emulate the decision-making abilities of human experts in specific domains. Systems like MYCIN, designed for medical diagnosis, and DENDRAL, for chemical analysis, showcased the practical applications of AI in specialized fields.

The turn of the century brought about a shift towards machine learning, a subfield of AI that focuses on developing algorithms that enable machines to learn from data. Breakthroughs in neural networks, particularly deep learning, revolutionized the field. The creation of convolutional neural networks (CNNs) and recurrent neural networks (RNNs) allowed for significant improvements in image and speech recognition.

Current State of AI Technology:

Today, AI encompasses a wide range of technologies, including machine learning, natural language processing, computer vision, and robotics. These technologies are integrated into various applications, from virtual assistants like Siri and Alexa to autonomous vehicles and advanced diagnostic tools in healthcare.

Machine learning algorithms, particularly those based on deep learning, have achieved remarkable success in tasks such as image and speech recognition, natural language understanding, and game playing. AI systems like AlphaGo, developed by DeepMind, have demonstrated the ability to surpass human experts in complex games like Go, showcasing the potential of AI in strategic decision-making.

Natural language processing (NLP) has also seen significant advancements, with models like OpenAI's GPT-3 capable of generating coherent and contextually relevant text. These models have applications in chatbots, language translation, and content generation, among others.

The integration of AI into various industries has led to increased efficiency, accuracy, and innovation. In healthcare,

AI-powered diagnostic tools assist doctors in identifying diseases and recommending treatments. In finance, AI algorithms analyze market trends and detect fraudulent activities. In transportation, autonomous vehicles are being developed to enhance road safety and reduce traffic congestion.

As AI technology continues to evolve, its potential applications expand, promising further advancements and disruptions across multiple sectors. The legal industry, traditionally known for its reliance on human expertise and judgment, is now beginning to explore the transformative potential of AI.

III. AI in the Legal System: An Overview

The legal system, with its vast amounts of data, complex regulations, and need for precise analysis, presents a unique opportunity for the application of artificial intelligence. AI tools have the potential to enhance various aspects of legal practice, from research and analysis to decision-making and client interaction. This section provides an overview of the current applications of AI in the legal system, highlighting the benefits and challenges of these technologies.

Introduction to AI Applications in Law:

Artificial intelligence has the capability to process large volumes of data quickly and accurately, making it an ideal tool for the legal industry. Legal professionals deal with extensive documents, case law, statutes, and regulations, which require thorough analysis and interpretation. AI can assist in automating repetitive tasks, extracting relevant information, and providing insights that would be time-consuming for humans to achieve.

Examples of AI Tools Used in the Legal System:

1. Legal Research Platforms: AI-powered legal research platforms, such as LexisNexis and Westlaw Edge, use natural language processing and machine learning algorithms to analyze legal documents, statutes, and case law. These platforms can quickly identify relevant precedents and provide summaries, significantly reducing the time required for legal research.

2. Predictive Analytics: AI tools like Premonition and Ravel Law utilize predictive analytics to forecast the outcomes of legal cases based on historical data. By analyzing past rulings, judge behavior, and case specifics, these tools provide insights into the likely success of a case, helping lawyers strategize and

make informed decisions.

3. Contract Analysis and Drafting: AI-driven contract analysis tools, such as Kira Systems and LawGeex, automate the review and analysis of contracts. These tools can identify key clauses, highlight potential risks, and ensure compliance with legal standards. Additionally, AI can assist in drafting contracts by suggesting language based on predefined templates and legal requirements.

4. Document Review and E-Discovery: AI-powered e-discovery tools, such as Relativity and Everlaw, streamline the process of reviewing and categorizing large volumes of documents for litigation. These tools use machine learning algorithms to identify relevant documents, reduce redundancy, and prioritize key information, making the discovery process more efficient and cost-effective.

Benefits and Challenges of AI in Legal Practice

Benefits of AI in Legal Practice

1. Increased Efficiency: AI-driven tools can process vast amounts of data quickly and accurately. Tasks that traditionally

took hours or days, such as document review and legal research, can now be completed in a fraction of the time. This increased efficiency allows legal professionals to focus on more complex and strategic aspects of their work.

2. Cost Reduction: By automating routine and labor-intensive tasks, AI reduces the need for extensive manual labor, which translates to lower operational costs for law firms. This cost reduction can be passed on to clients, making legal services more affordable and accessible.

3. Enhanced Accuracy: AI systems, particularly those based on machine learning and natural language processing, can analyze legal documents with high precision, identifying relevant information and potential risks that might be overlooked by human reviewers. This reduces the likelihood of errors and improves the overall quality of legal work.

4. Predictive Analytics: AI can analyze historical case data to predict outcomes of current cases. This capability helps lawyers assess the strengths and weaknesses of a case, develop better strategies, and provide clients with more informed advice regarding the potential success of their legal actions.

5. Improved Access to Justice: AI-powered legal services, such as virtual legal assistants and chatbots, can provide basic legal information and guidance to individuals who may not have the means to consult a lawyer. This democratizes access to legal information, empowering people to understand their rights and options.

6. Streamlined Legal Processes: AI can automate various administrative tasks, such as scheduling, billing, and case management. This streamlining of processes reduces administrative burdens on legal professionals, allowing them to allocate more time to substantive legal work.

Challenges of AI in Legal Practice

1. Bias and Fairness: AI systems are only as unbiased as the data they are trained on. If the training data contains biases, the AI can perpetuate and even exacerbate these biases in its outputs. This is particularly concerning in legal contexts, where biased decisions can have significant repercussions on justice and fairness.

2. Loss of Jobs: The automation of routine legal tasks poses a

threat to jobs traditionally held by paralegals and junior lawyers. As AI takes over these roles, there is a risk of job displacement, necessitating a shift in the skill sets required for legal professionals.

3. Ethical Concerns: The use of AI in legal practice raises ethical questions about the role of human judgment and accountability. Decisions made by AI systems may lack the nuanced understanding and moral reasoning that human lawyers bring to their work. Ensuring ethical oversight and maintaining the integrity of legal practice are critical challenges.

4. Data Privacy and Security: Legal work often involves sensitive and confidential information. The use of AI systems necessitates stringent data privacy and security measures to protect this information from breaches and unauthorized access. Ensuring compliance with data protection regulations is paramount.

5. Regulatory and Legal Compliance: The integration of AI in legal practice is subject to evolving regulations and legal standards. Law firms must navigate these regulatory landscapes, ensuring that their use of AI complies with relevant

laws and guidelines. This requires continuous monitoring and adaptation to new legal requirements.

6. Dependence on Technology: Overreliance on AI can lead to a decrease in critical thinking and problem-solving skills among legal professionals. It is essential to strike a balance between leveraging AI's capabilities and maintaining the fundamental skills that underpin legal practice.

Conclusion

AI offers significant benefits to the legal profession, including increased efficiency, cost reduction, enhanced accuracy, predictive analytics, improved access to justice, and streamlined processes. However, these advantages are accompanied by challenges such as bias, job displacement, ethical concerns, data privacy, regulatory compliance, and dependence on technology. As AI continues to evolve, it is crucial for legal professionals to navigate these challenges thoughtfully, ensuring that the integration of AI enhances rather than undermines the principles of justice and fairness in the legal system.

IV. AI and Legal Research

How AI Enhances Legal Research

Artificial Intelligence (AI) has revolutionized many aspects of modern life, and legal research is no exception. Traditional legal research methods, which involve sifting through vast amounts of case law, statutes, regulations, and legal commentaries, are time-consuming and labor-intensive. AI enhances legal research by automating these processes, improving accuracy, and providing predictive analytics.

1. Automating Document Review and Data Extraction: AI algorithms, particularly those using natural language processing (NLP), can quickly scan and analyze large volumes of legal documents. They extract relevant information, such as key case details, legal principles, and precedents, significantly reducing the time lawyers spend on manual document review. This automation enables legal professionals to focus on higher-level analysis and strategic decision-making.

2. Improving Accuracy and Consistency: Human error is an inevitable part of manual legal research. AI systems, however, maintain a high level of accuracy and consistency in analyzing legal texts. By training AI on comprehensive and high-quality

datasets, these systems can identify and interpret legal nuances with precision, minimizing the risk of oversight or error.

3. Predictive Analytics and Case Outcome Prediction: One of the most transformative applications of AI in legal research is its ability to predict case outcomes. By analyzing historical case data and identifying patterns, AI can provide insights into how similar cases have been decided. This predictive capability assists lawyers in assessing the likelihood of success in a case, guiding their strategies and helping manage client expectations.

4. Natural Language Processing (NLP): NLP enables AI to understand and interpret human language, making it possible to query legal databases using natural language queries. Instead of using specific keywords or Boolean searches, lawyers can ask questions in plain English, and the AI system will understand the context and provide relevant results. This user-friendly approach democratizes access to legal information, making it easier for lawyers to find what they need.

5. Enhanced Research Speed: AI-powered tools can process information at speeds far beyond human capability. This rapid processing is particularly beneficial in legal research, where timely access to information can be critical. Lawyers can

quickly retrieve relevant cases, statutes, and legal articles, allowing them to build stronger arguments and respond more effectively to legal challenges.

6. Comprehensive Legal Insights: AI can integrate and analyze data from various sources, including case law, statutes, regulations, legal journals, and news articles. This comprehensive approach provides lawyers with a broader perspective on legal issues, helping them understand trends, identify emerging legal challenges, and stay informed about recent developments in their areas of practice.

Case Studies of AI in Legal Research

1. ROSS Intelligence

ROSS Intelligence, powered by IBM's Watson, is one of the pioneering AI platforms in legal research. It uses NLP and machine learning to understand legal queries and provide precise answers. Law firms like BakerHostetler have implemented ROSS to streamline their bankruptcy practice. ROSS helps lawyers quickly find relevant case law, statutory provisions, and legal precedents. By automating these research tasks, ROSS has significantly reduced the time spent on legal research, allowing lawyers to focus on more strategic activities.

2. LexisNexis and Lex Machina

LexisNexis, a leader in legal research solutions, acquired Lex Machina to enhance its AI capabilities. Lex Machina uses AI to mine litigation data and provide insights into legal trends, case outcomes, and judge behavior. Law firms and corporate legal departments use Lex Machina to predict the outcomes of patent litigation cases, develop litigation strategies, and even decide whether to settle or proceed to trial. This AI-driven approach has transformed how lawyers approach patent litigation, providing them with data-driven insights that were previously unavailable.

3. Westlaw Edge

Thomson Reuters' Westlaw Edge is an AI-powered legal research platform that combines NLP, machine learning, and advanced analytics. Westlaw Edge offers features like WestSearch Plus, which allows lawyers to ask legal questions in natural language and receive accurate results. It also includes the Litigation Analytics tool, which provides data on judges, courts, attorneys, and law firms, helping lawyers craft more effective litigation strategies. Law firms using Westlaw Edge report significant time savings and improved research accuracy, enhancing their overall productivity.

4. Casetext and CARA

Casetext is another AI-driven legal research tool that uses a technology called CARA (Case Analysis Research Assistant). CARA analyzes legal briefs and identifies relevant case law that might have been overlooked. This tool is particularly useful for identifying cases that are directly on point, helping lawyers build stronger arguments. Casetext's AI-driven approach has gained popularity among solo practitioners and small law firms, who benefit from its affordability and efficiency.

5. Ravel Law

Ravel Law, acquired by LexisNexis, leverages AI to provide visualizations of case law data, making it easier for lawyers to identify patterns and relationships between cases. Its Judge Analytics feature offers insights into how judges have ruled on similar issues in the past, helping lawyers tailor their arguments to specific judges. By integrating AI with data visualization,

Ravel Law has made legal research more intuitive and accessible.

Future Prospects of AI in Legal Research

1. Advanced Predictive Analytics

The future of AI in legal research promises even more advanced predictive analytics. As AI algorithms continue to improve, their ability to predict case outcomes with higher accuracy will become a game-changer. Lawyers will be able to assess the strengths and weaknesses of a case with greater confidence, leading to better-informed decisions about whether to proceed to trial, settle, or explore alternative dispute resolution methods.

Enhanced NLP Capabilities

Advancements in NLP will further enhance AI's ability to understand and interpret legal language. AI systems will become more adept at handling complex legal queries, recognizing subtle nuances, and providing precise answers. This will make legal research even more efficient and user-friendly, reducing the time and effort required to find relevant information.

3. Integration with Blockchain Technology

The integration of AI with blockchain technology has the potential to revolutionize legal research. Blockchain's immutable and transparent nature can enhance the reliability and traceability of legal documents and case law. AI can leverage blockchain data to verify the authenticity of legal records, track changes, and ensure the integrity of information used in legal research.

4. Personalized Legal Research

AI will enable personalized legal research tailored to the specific needs and preferences of individual lawyers. By analyzing a lawyer's past research patterns, preferences, and areas of expertise, AI systems can provide customized recommendations and insights. This personalization will improve the efficiency and effectiveness of legal research, allowing lawyers to access the most relevant information quickly.

5. AI-Assisted Drafting and Analysis

The future will see AI playing a more significant role in drafting legal documents and conducting complex legal analyses. AI systems will be able to generate legal briefs, contracts, and other documents, reducing the time and effort required for manual drafting. Additionally, AI will assist lawyers in conducting in-depth analyses of legal issues, providing comprehensive insights and recommendations.

6. Augmented Reality (AR) and Virtual Reality (VR) in Legal Research

The integration of AI with AR and VR technologies holds exciting prospects for legal research. Lawyers could use AR glasses to overlay case law and legal information onto physical documents, enhancing their research experience. VR environments could simulate courtrooms and legal scenarios, allowing lawyers to practice and refine their arguments in realistic settings. This immersive approach will transform how legal research and preparation are conducted.

7. Ethical and Regulatory Considerations

As AI continues to evolve, ethical and regulatory

considerations will play a crucial role in shaping its future in legal research. Ensuring the fairness, transparency, and accountability of AI systems will be paramount. Legal professionals, policymakers, and technologists must collaborate to establish guidelines and standards that govern the use of AI in legal research, protecting the integrity of the legal system and the rights of individuals.

Conclusion

AI has already begun to transform legal research, offering significant benefits in terms of efficiency, accuracy, and predictive capabilities. Case studies of AI applications like ROSS Intelligence, Lex Machina, Westlaw Edge, Casetext, and Ravel Law demonstrate the profound impact of AI on legal practice. The future prospects of AI in legal research are promising, with advancements in predictive analytics, NLP, blockchain integration, personalized research, AI-assisted drafting, and AR/VR technologies.

As AI continues to evolve, it is essential for the legal profession to embrace these innovations while addressing the ethical and regulatory challenges that accompany them. By leveraging AI's capabilities, legal professionals can enhance their research processes, improve access to justice, and ultimately contribute to a more efficient and effective legal system. The integration of AI in legal research marks a significant step forward, paving the way for a future where technology and human expertise work hand in hand to advance the practice of law.

V. AI in Predictive Analytics

Introduction to Predictive Analytics in Law

Predictive analytics involves the use of statistical techniques, machine learning algorithms, and data mining to analyze historical data and make predictions about future outcomes. In the legal field, predictive analytics harnesses the power of AI to forecast the likely results of legal disputes, identify trends, and provide strategic insights. This application of AI is transforming how lawyers approach case management, litigation strategy, and client counseling.

Predictive analytics in law leverages vast amounts of data from past cases, legal precedents, and other relevant sources. AI algorithms analyze this data to identify patterns and correlations that can inform predictions about case outcomes, judge behavior, and the success of legal arguments. This capability allows lawyers to make data-driven decisions, enhancing their ability to advise clients, assess risks, and develop effective legal strategies.

The integration of predictive analytics into legal practice offers numerous benefits, including increased efficiency, improved accuracy, and better resource allocation. However, it also raises important ethical and legal questions regarding fairness, accountability, and the potential for bias. This essay explores the impact of AI-driven predictive analytics on the legal profession, examining case studies and addressing the ethical and legal implications.

Case Studies of Predictive Analytics

1. Lex Machina

Lex Machina, a subsidiary of LexisNexis, is a leading example of predictive analytics in the legal industry. The platform uses AI to analyze litigation data from federal courts, providing insights into case outcomes, judge behavior, and attorney performance. Lex Machina's tools help legal professionals assess the likelihood of success in specific jurisdictions, identify winning legal strategies, and evaluate the strengths and weaknesses of their cases.

One notable application of Lex Machina is in patent litigation. By analyzing historical patent case data, the platform can predict the outcomes of new cases, helping lawyers decide whether to pursue litigation or settle. This predictive capability enables law firms to make more informed decisions, optimize their litigation strategies, and manage client expectations more effectively.

2. Premonition

Premonition is another AI-powered platform that utilizes predictive analytics to forecast case outcomes. The system collects and analyzes data from court records, identifying patterns that can predict the success of legal arguments and the behavior of judges and opposing counsel. Premonition's predictive models provide insights into the likelihood of winning a case, the duration of litigation, and the potential costs involved.

Law firms use Premonition to gain a competitive edge by tailoring their strategies based on data-driven insights. For example, by understanding a judge's historical rulings on similar cases, lawyers can craft arguments that are more likely to resonate with that judge. This strategic advantage can significantly improve the chances of a favorable outcome.

3. Ravel Law

Ravel Law, now part of LexisNexis, offers AI-driven tools that combine legal research with predictive analytics. The platform's Judge Analytics feature provides detailed insights into how judges have ruled on various issues in the past. By analyzing judicial behavior, Ravel Law helps lawyers predict how a judge might rule in a particular case, allowing them to adjust their strategies accordingly.

In one case study, a law firm used Ravel Law to analyze a judge's historical rulings on employment discrimination cases. The analysis revealed that the judge tended to favor plaintiffs in cases involving specific types of discrimination claims. Armed with this information, the firm's lawyers tailored their arguments to align with the judge's tendencies, ultimately achieving a favorable verdict for their client.

4. Legalist

Legalist is a litigation finance company that uses predictive analytics to evaluate the potential success of legal cases. By analyzing data on case outcomes, judge behavior, and other relevant factors, Legalist assesses the likelihood of winning a case and provides funding to plaintiffs with strong prospects. This data-driven approach allows Legalist to make informed investment decisions, supporting cases with a higher probability of success.

One example of Legalist's application involved a small business suing a larger corporation for breach of contract. Using predictive analytics, Legalist determined that the small business had a strong case and provided the necessary funding to pursue litigation. The data-driven decision paid off, as the small business ultimately won the case and received a substantial settlement.

Ethical and Legal Implications

The integration of predictive analytics into legal practice offers significant benefits, but it also raises several ethical and legal concerns that must be carefully considered.

1. Bias and Fairness

One of the primary ethical concerns with predictive analytics is the potential for bias. AI algorithms are trained on historical data, which may contain biases related to race, gender, socioeconomic status, and other factors. If these biases are not addressed, predictive models can perpetuate and even exacerbate existing inequalities in the legal system. Ensuring fairness and transparency in AI-driven predictive analytics is crucial to maintaining the integrity of the legal process.

To mitigate bias, developers of predictive analytics tools must carefully select and preprocess training data, implement bias detection and correction mechanisms, and continuously monitor the performance of their models. Legal professionals using these tools should also be aware of the potential for bias and critically evaluate the predictions they receive.

2. Accountability and Transparency

Predictive analytics introduces questions of accountability and transparency in legal decision-making. When lawyers rely on AI-generated predictions, it can be challenging to understand the rationale behind those predictions. This lack of transparency, often referred to as the "black box" problem, can undermine trust in AI systems and complicate efforts to hold parties accountable for their decisions.

To address this issue, developers should prioritize the creation of explainable AI models that provide insights into how predictions are made. Legal professionals should also be trained to interpret and contextualize AI-generated predictions, ensuring that they use these tools as aids rather than replacements for human judgment.

3. Privacy and Data Security

The use of predictive analytics in law requires access to vast amounts of sensitive data, including court records, legal documents, and personal information. Ensuring the privacy and security of this data is paramount. Unauthorized access, data breaches, and misuse of data can have severe consequences for individuals and organizations involved in legal proceedings.

Legal professionals and AI developers must implement robust data protection measures, comply with relevant privacy regulations, and establish protocols for secure data handling. Additionally, clear policies should be in place to govern data access and usage, ensuring that only authorized personnel can interact with sensitive information.

4. Legal and Ethical Standards

The rapid adoption of AI-driven predictive analytics in law necessitates the development of new legal and ethical standards. Regulatory bodies, legal associations, and policymakers must collaborate to establish guidelines that govern the use of AI in legal practice. These standards should address issues such as bias, transparency, accountability, and data privacy, providing a framework for the ethical and responsible use of predictive analytics.

Moreover, legal professionals must stay informed about evolving best practices and legal requirements related to AI. Continuing education and professional development programs can help lawyers understand the ethical and legal implications of predictive analytics and ensure that they use these tools responsibly.

5. Impact on the Legal Profession

The integration of predictive analytics into legal practice has the potential to reshape the legal profession. While these tools can enhance efficiency and effectiveness, they also raise questions about the future role of lawyers and the skills required for success in a data-driven environment.

As predictive analytics becomes more prevalent, legal education and training programs must adapt to prepare future lawyers for the evolving landscape. This includes teaching data literacy, ethical considerations, and the effective use of AI tools in legal practice. Lawyers must also develop a critical understanding of AI's limitations and ensure that they continue to play a central role in interpreting and applying the law.

Conclusion

AI-driven predictive analytics is transforming the legal profession, offering significant benefits in terms of efficiency, accuracy, and strategic decision-making. Case studies of platforms like Lex Machina, Premonition, Ravel Law, and Legalist demonstrate the profound impact of predictive analytics on legal practice, from predicting case outcomes to tailoring litigation strategies.

However, the integration of predictive analytics also raises important ethical and legal implications, including concerns about bias, accountability, transparency, privacy, and the future of the legal profession. Addressing these challenges requires a collaborative effort among developers, legal professionals, and policymakers to establish guidelines and best practices that ensure the ethical and responsible use of AI in law.

By navigating these complexities thoughtfully, the legal profession can harness the power of predictive analytics to enhance access to justice, improve the efficiency of legal processes, and ultimately contribute to a more equitable and effective legal system. As AI continues to evolve, its role in predictive analytics will undoubtedly expand, offering new opportunities and challenges for the legal community.

VI. AI in Contract Analysis and Drafting

Role of AI in Contract Analysis

AI plays a transformative role in contract analysis by automating and enhancing the accuracy of tasks traditionally performed by legal professionals. Contract analysis involves reviewing, extracting, and interpreting critical information from legal documents, a process that can be time-consuming and prone to human error. AI-driven tools utilize natural language processing (NLP) and machine learning algorithms to streamline this process, providing several key benefits:

1. Efficiency and Speed: AI can analyze large volumes of contracts rapidly, significantly reducing the time required for review. This is particularly useful for businesses dealing with numerous contracts, such as mergers and acquisitions, real estate transactions, and vendor agreements.

2. Accuracy and Consistency: AI systems are capable of consistently identifying and extracting relevant clauses, terms, and conditions from contracts. This minimizes the risk of oversight or misinterpretation that can occur with manual review.

3. Risk Mitigation: AI-driven contract analysis tools can identify potential risks and compliance issues within contracts. By flagging problematic clauses and deviations from standard terms, these tools help legal teams address issues proactively.

4. Standardization: AI can assist in standardizing contract language and formats, ensuring that all contracts adhere to organizational policies and legal requirements. This uniformity

simplifies contract management and reduces the likelihood of disputes.

5. Cost Reduction: Automating contract analysis reduces the need for extensive manual labor, leading to cost savings for law firms and corporate legal departments. This efficiency allows legal professionals to focus on higher-value tasks, such as negotiation and strategic planning.

Examples of AI-Driven Contract Tools

1. Kira Systems

Kira Systems is a leading AI-powered contract analysis tool that uses machine learning to identify and extract information from contracts and other legal documents. It can handle various types of documents, including leases, NDAs, and purchase agreements. Kira's technology improves over time by learning from user input, making it increasingly accurate and efficient. Law firms and corporations use Kira to streamline due diligence processes, identify risks, and ensure compliance with regulatory requirements.

2. Luminance

Luminance leverages advanced machine learning algorithms to provide insights into contract data. Its platform can analyze and categorize contracts, highlighting key clauses, anomalies, and areas of interest. Luminance is particularly effective in managing large-scale document reviews, such as those required during mergers and acquisitions. By offering visualizations and summaries of contract data, Luminance helps legal teams make informed decisions quickly.

3. eBrevia

eBrevia, powered by AI and NLP, is designed to improve the accuracy and speed of contract review and extraction. It can identify and extract over 200 types of data points from contracts, including financial terms, obligations, and expiration dates. eBrevia's platform integrates with existing document management systems, making it easy for legal teams to incorporate AI-driven analysis into their workflows. The tool is used for various applications, including due diligence, lease abstraction, and regulatory compliance.

4. LawGeex

LawGeex uses AI to automate the review and approval of contracts. Its platform compares incoming contracts against predefined policies and standards, identifying deviations and suggesting revisions. LawGeex's technology is particularly useful for managing routine contracts, such as NDAs and employment agreements, ensuring that they comply with organizational guidelines. By automating these tasks, LawGeex reduces the workload on legal teams and speeds up contract turnaround times.

5. ROSS Intelligence

Originally developed for legal research, ROSS Intelligence has expanded its capabilities to include contract analysis. Using advanced NLP, ROSS can read and understand contract language, identifying key clauses and potential issues. It assists lawyers in drafting and revising contracts by suggesting language based on best practices and legal precedents. ROSS's AI-driven approach enhances the efficiency and accuracy of contract management processes.

Future Trends and Impact on Legal Practice

1. Integration with Blockchain Technology

One of the emerging trends in AI-driven contract analysis is the integration with blockchain technology. Smart contracts, which are self-executing contracts with the terms directly written into code, leverage blockchain to ensure security, transparency, and immutability. AI can enhance the functionality of smart contracts by automating the review and validation of contract terms before they are executed on the blockchain. This integration promises to revolutionize contract management, reducing the need for intermediaries and increasing trust in digital transactions.

2. Enhanced Natural Language Processing (NLP)

As NLP technology advances, AI-driven contract tools will become even more sophisticated in understanding and interpreting complex legal language. Improved NLP capabilities will allow these tools to handle nuanced and context-specific contract terms with greater accuracy. This will further reduce the reliance on human review and increase the efficiency of contract analysis and drafting.

3. Predictive Analytics and Risk Assessment

The future of AI in contract analysis will see greater use of predictive analytics to assess the risks associated with contractual terms. By analyzing historical data and identifying patterns, AI can predict potential issues and outcomes related to specific clauses. This predictive capability will help legal professionals make more informed decisions during contract negotiation and drafting, ultimately reducing the likelihood of disputes and litigation.

4. Personalized Contract Drafting

AI-driven tools will increasingly offer personalized contract drafting capabilities, tailoring contract templates to the specific needs and preferences of individual clients or organizations. By analyzing past contracts and user inputs, AI systems can generate customized contract drafts that align with specific legal and business requirements. This personalization will enhance the efficiency and effectiveness of contract management processes.

5. Increased Accessibility and Adoption

As AI technology becomes more accessible and user-friendly, a wider range of legal professionals and organizations will adopt AI-driven contract analysis tools. Smaller law firms and in-house legal teams, which may have previously lacked the resources to implement advanced technology, will benefit from AI's capabilities. This democratization of AI in legal practice will level the playing field and enable more efficient and effective contract management across the industry.

6. Ethical and Regulatory Considerations

The increasing use of AI in contract analysis and drafting raises important ethical and regulatory considerations. Ensuring the transparency and accountability of AI-driven tools will be crucial in maintaining trust and integrity in the legal process. Legal professionals and technology developers must collaborate to establish guidelines and best practices for the ethical use of AI in contract management. This includes addressing issues related to data privacy, bias, and the potential for over-reliance on automated systems.

Conclusion

AI has already begun to transform contract analysis and drafting, offering significant benefits in terms of efficiency, accuracy, and risk mitigation. Tools like Kira Systems, Luminance, eBrevia, LawGeex, and ROSS Intelligence exemplify the capabilities of AI-driven contract management solutions. These tools streamline the review and extraction of contract data, identify potential risks, and ensure compliance with legal and organizational standards.

Looking to the future, the integration of AI with blockchain technology, advancements in NLP, predictive analytics, personalized contract drafting, increased accessibility, and ethical considerations will shape the evolution of AI in contract analysis and drafting. As AI continues to advance, it will play an increasingly central role in legal practice, enabling legal professionals to manage contracts more efficiently, make informed decisions, and ultimately provide better service to their clients.

The impact of AI on contract management will be profound, driving innovation and transforming the way legal work is conducted. By embracing these technological advancements, the legal profession can harness the full potential of AI to enhance the efficiency, accuracy, and effectiveness of contract analysis and drafting.

VII. AI in Judicial Decision-Making

Overview of AI in Judicial Processes

Artificial Intelligence (AI) has progressively permeated various aspects of the legal system, including judicial decision-making. AI in judicial processes refers to the use of machine learning algorithms, natural language processing (NLP), and data analytics to assist judges and legal professionals in making more informed and consistent decisions. The integration of AI aims to enhance efficiency, reduce biases, and improve the overall administration of justice.

AI technologies can analyze vast amounts of legal data, including past case law, statutes, regulations, and legal opinions. By identifying patterns and drawing insights from this data, AI can provide recommendations, predict case outcomes, and even draft preliminary rulings. These capabilities can significantly aid judges in handling their caseloads more efficiently and ensuring that similar cases receive similar treatment.

.

Case Studies and Examples

1. COMPAS (Correctional Offender Management Profiling for Alternative Sanctions)

One of the earliest and most well-known examples of AI in judicial decision-making is the COMPAS system, used in the United States to assess the risk of recidivism among defendants. COMPAS uses a variety of factors, including criminal history, personal background, and social behavior, to predict the likelihood that an offender will re-offend. Judges use these risk assessments to make decisions about bail, sentencing, and parole.

However, COMPAS has been the subject of significant controversy. A 2016 investigation by ProPublica revealed that the system was biased against African American defendants, who were more likely to be incorrectly classified as high risk compared to their white counterparts. This case highlights both the potential and the pitfalls of AI in judicial decision-making.

2. The Estonian e-Justice System

Estonia is at the forefront of integrating AI into its judicial system. The country has implemented an e-Justice system that includes AI tools to assist judges with case management and legal research. One notable initiative is the use of an AI judge to adjudicate small claims disputes. The AI judge can handle claims up to €7,000, analyzing documents and evidence submitted electronically to render decisions.

This system has streamlined the adjudication process, reducing the backlog of cases and speeding up the delivery of justice. It also frees up human judges to focus on more complex cases, thereby improving overall judicial efficiency.

3. HART (Harm Assessment Risk Tool)

In the UK, the Durham Constabulary has employed an AI tool known as HART to predict the risk of future offending. HART uses data from police records to classify individuals as low, medium, or high risk of committing a future crime. This information helps law enforcement and judicial officials make more informed decisions about bail and sentencing.

HART has shown promising results in accurately predicting low-risk individuals, allowing for more targeted interventions. However, like COMPAS, it also faces scrutiny regarding potential biases and the ethical implications of its use.

4. China's Smart Court System

China has been rapidly advancing its use of AI in the judicial system, with the implementation of the Smart Court initiative. This system integrates AI to assist judges with case processing, evidence evaluation, and legal research. One of the most significant aspects is the use of AI to generate draft judgments based on case data and legal principles.

In Zhejiang Province, AI tools have been used to handle cases related to traffic violations and minor civil disputes. These AI-driven decisions are then reviewed and finalized by human judges. The Smart Court system has improved efficiency, reduced case backlogs, and standardized judicial procedures across the province.

Ethical Concerns and Legal Ramifications

While AI offers significant benefits in judicial decision-making, its implementation raises several ethical and legal concerns that must be addressed to ensure fairness and justice.

1. Bias and Fairness

One of the primary ethical concerns with AI in judicial processes is the potential for bias. AI algorithms are trained on historical data, which may reflect existing biases within the legal system. If not properly addressed, these biases can be perpetuated or even amplified by AI systems. The COMPAS case is a prime example of how biased data can lead to unfair outcomes, particularly for minority groups.

Ensuring fairness in AI systems requires rigorous testing, validation, and ongoing monitoring. It is crucial to use diverse and representative data sets, implement bias detection and correction mechanisms, and maintain transparency in how AI models are developed and used.

2. Transparency and Accountability

AI systems often operate as "black boxes," making it difficult to understand how they arrive at specific decisions or recommendations. This lack of transparency can undermine trust in the judicial system and complicate efforts to hold parties accountable for their decisions. In the context of judicial decision-making, it is essential that AI tools provide explanations for their outputs and that judges understand how to interpret and use these recommendations.

Establishing clear guidelines and standards for the development and deployment of AI in judicial processes can help ensure transparency and accountability. Legal professionals and technologists must work together to create explainable AI models and educate judges on their proper use.

3. Data Privacy and Security

The use of AI in judicial decision-making involves processing vast amounts of sensitive data, including personal information about defendants, victims, and witnesses. Protecting this data from unauthorized access, breaches, and misuse is paramount. Data privacy laws and regulations must be strictly adhered to, and robust security measures must be implemented to safeguard sensitive information.

Legal frameworks should be updated to address the unique challenges posed by AI, ensuring that data privacy and security standards are upheld in all AI-driven judicial processes.

4. Due Process and Human Oversight

The integration of AI in judicial decision-making must not undermine the principles of due process and human oversight. Defendants have the right to a fair and impartial hearing, which includes the opportunity to challenge evidence and present their case. AI systems should be used as tools to assist judges rather than replace them, ensuring that human judgment and legal expertise remain central to the judicial process.

Judges must retain the final authority in making decisions, with AI providing support and recommendations. This balance between AI assistance and human oversight is crucial to maintaining the integrity and legitimacy of the judicial system.

5. Legal and Ethical Standards

The rapid adoption of AI in judicial decision-making necessitates the development of comprehensive legal and ethical standards. These standards should address issues such as bias, transparency, accountability, data privacy, and due process. International cooperation and collaboration among legal professionals, policymakers, and technologists are essential to establish best practices and guidelines for the ethical use of AI in judicial processes.

Professional associations, such as bar associations and judicial councils, can play a vital role in developing these standards and providing education and training to judges and legal professionals on the ethical use of AI.

Conclusion

AI has the potential to revolutionize judicial decision-making by enhancing efficiency, consistency, and accuracy. Case studies from the United States, Estonia, the UK, and China demonstrate the diverse applications and benefits of AI in judicial processes. However, the integration of AI also raises significant ethical and legal concerns that must be carefully addressed.

Ensuring fairness, transparency, accountability, data privacy, and due process are critical to the ethical use of AI in judicial decision-making. By establishing clear guidelines and standards, promoting collaboration among stakeholders, and maintaining human oversight, the legal system can harness the power of AI to improve the administration of justice while upholding the principles of fairness and integrity.

4. Due Process and Human Oversight

The integration of AI in judicial decision-making must not undermine the principles of due process and human oversight. Defendants have the right to a fair and impartial hearing, which includes the opportunity to challenge evidence and present their case. AI systems should be used as tools to assist judges rather than replace them, ensuring that human judgment and legal expertise remain central to the judicial process.

Judges must retain the final authority in making decisions, with AI providing support and recommendations. This balance between AI assistance and human oversight is crucial to maintaining the integrity and legitimacy of the judicial system.

5. Legal and Ethical Standards

The rapid adoption of AI in judicial decision-making necessitates the development of comprehensive legal and ethical standards. These standards should address issues such as bias, transparency, accountability, data privacy, and due process. International cooperation and collaboration among legal professionals, policymakers, and technologists are essential to establish best practices and guidelines for the ethical use of AI in judicial processes.

Professional associations, such as bar associations and judicial councils, can play a vital role in developing these standards and providing education and training to judges and legal professionals on the ethical use of AI.

Conclusion

AI has the potential to revolutionize judicial decision-making by enhancing efficiency, consistency, and accuracy. Case studies from the United States, Estonia, the UK, and China demonstrate the diverse applications and benefits of AI in judicial processes. However, the integration of AI also raises significant ethical and legal concerns that must be carefully addressed.

Ensuring fairness, transparency, accountability, data privacy, and due process are critical to the ethical use of AI in judicial decision-making. By establishing clear guidelines and standards, promoting collaboration among stakeholders, and maintaining human oversight, the legal system can harness the power of AI to improve the administration of justice while upholding the principles of fairness and integrity.

The future of AI in judicial decision-making holds great promise, but it requires a thoughtful and balanced approach to navigate the complexities and challenges it presents. Through careful implementation and ongoing evaluation, AI can be a powerful tool to support judges and enhance the judicial process, ultimately contributing to a more just and efficient legal system.

VIII. AI and Legal Ethics

Ethical Considerations of Using AI in Law

The integration of Artificial Intelligence (AI) into the legal field presents numerous ethical considerations that must be carefully addressed to ensure the fair and just application of the law. As AI technologies become more prevalent in legal practice, it is crucial to examine the ethical implications related to bias, transparency, accountability, and the potential impact on the legal profession.

1. Bias and Fairness

One of the most significant ethical concerns with AI in law is the potential for bias. AI systems are trained on historical data, which may contain inherent biases related to race, gender, socioeconomic status, and other factors. If these biases are not adequately addressed, AI-driven legal tools can perpetuate and even exacerbate existing inequalities within the legal system.

To mitigate bias, it is essential to ensure that AI models are trained on diverse and representative data sets. Developers should implement robust bias detection and correction mechanisms and continuously monitor the performance of AI systems to identify and rectify any biases that may arise. Additionally, involving diverse teams in the development and testing of AI tools can help to uncover and address potential biases.

2. Transparency and Explainability

AI systems often operate as "black boxes," making it difficult to understand how they arrive at specific decisions or recommendations. This lack of transparency can undermine trust in AI-driven legal tools and pose challenges to accountability. In the legal context, it is crucial that AI systems provide clear and explainable outputs, allowing legal professionals to understand and interpret the reasoning behind

The future of AI in judicial decision-making holds great promise, but it requires a thoughtful and balanced approach to navigate the complexities and challenges it presents. Through careful implementation and ongoing evaluation, AI can be a powerful tool to support judges and enhance the judicial process, ultimately contributing to a more just and efficient legal system.

VIII. AI and Legal Ethics

Ethical Considerations of Using AI in Law

The integration of Artificial Intelligence (AI) into the legal field presents numerous ethical considerations that must be carefully addressed to ensure the fair and just application of the law. As AI technologies become more prevalent in legal practice, it is crucial to examine the ethical implications related to bias, transparency, accountability, and the potential impact on the legal profession.

1. Bias and Fairness

One of the most significant ethical concerns with AI in law is the potential for bias. AI systems are trained on historical data, which may contain inherent biases related to race, gender, socioeconomic status, and other factors. If these biases are not adequately addressed, AI-driven legal tools can perpetuate and even exacerbate existing inequalities within the legal system.

To mitigate bias, it is essential to ensure that AI models are trained on diverse and representative data sets. Developers should implement robust bias detection and correction mechanisms and continuously monitor the performance of AI systems to identify and rectify any biases that may arise. Additionally, involving diverse teams in the development and testing of AI tools can help to uncover and address potential biases.

2. Transparency and Explainability

AI systems often operate as "black boxes," making it difficult to understand how they arrive at specific decisions or recommendations. This lack of transparency can undermine trust in AI-driven legal tools and pose challenges to accountability. In the legal context, it is crucial that AI systems provide clear and explainable outputs, allowing legal professionals to understand and interpret the reasoning behind

AI-generated recommendations.

Developers should prioritize the creation of explainable AI models that offer insights into how decisions are made. Legal professionals must be trained to critically evaluate AI outputs and integrate them into their decision-making processes. Transparent AI systems can enhance trust and ensure that AI is used responsibly within the legal profession.

3. Accountability and Responsibility

The use of AI in legal practice raises questions about accountability and responsibility. When AI systems are involved in legal decision-making, it can be challenging to determine who is accountable for the outcomes. Legal professionals must retain ultimate responsibility for decisions made with the assistance of AI, ensuring that human judgment and ethical considerations remain central to the process.

Clear guidelines and standards should be established to delineate the roles and responsibilities of AI developers, legal professionals, and other stakeholders. These guidelines should emphasize the importance of human oversight and the need for legal professionals to critically assess AI-generated recommendations before making final decisions.

4. Privacy and Data Security

The deployment of AI in legal practice involves the processing of vast amounts of sensitive data, including personal information about clients, defendants, and witnesses. Ensuring the privacy and security of this data is paramount. Unauthorized access, data breaches, and misuse of data can have severe consequences for individuals and organizations involved in legal proceedings.

Legal professionals and AI developers must implement robust data protection measures and comply with relevant privacy regulations. This includes secure data storage, encryption, access controls, and regular audits to ensure compliance with data protection standards. Additionally, clear policies should govern data access and usage, ensuring that only authorized personnel can interact with sensitive information.

5. Impact on the Legal Profession

The integration of AI into legal practice has the potential to reshape the legal profession. While AI can enhance efficiency and accuracy, it also raises concerns about job displacement and the changing roles of legal professionals. Paralegals and junior lawyers, who traditionally handle routine tasks, may face job displacement as AI automates these functions.

To address this issue, the legal profession must adapt by evolving roles and responsibilities and emphasizing the development of new skills. Legal education and training programs should incorporate AI and technology courses, preparing future lawyers for a landscape where technological proficiency is essential. By focusing on tasks that require human judgment, empathy, and ethical reasoning, legal professionals can continue to play a vital role in the legal system.

Regulatory Frameworks and Guidelines

As AI continues to transform the legal field, the development of regulatory frameworks and guidelines is essential to ensure the ethical and responsible use of AI technologies. Policymakers, legal associations, and other stakeholders must collaborate to establish comprehensive standards that address ethical considerations, promote transparency, and protect individual rights.

1. International Cooperation and Standards

The global nature of AI development and deployment necessitates international cooperation in establishing regulatory frameworks. International organizations, such as the European Union (EU), the United Nations (UN), and the Organisation for Economic Co-operation and Development (OECD), play a crucial role in developing guidelines and standards for the ethical use of AI.

For example, the EU has introduced the General Data Protection Regulation (GDPR), which includes provisions related to AI and data protection. The EU is also working on comprehensive AI legislation that emphasizes transparency, accountability, and ethical considerations. These international efforts provide a foundation for harmonizing AI regulations across jurisdictions, promoting ethical AI development and use globally.

2. National and Regional Regulations

In addition to international standards, individual countries and regions are developing their own regulatory frameworks for AI. These regulations address specific legal, cultural, and societal contexts, ensuring that AI deployment aligns with local values and legal traditions.

For instance, the United States has taken a more fragmented approach, with federal and state governments implementing various regulations and guidelines. The Federal Trade Commission (FTC) has issued guidelines on the ethical use of AI, emphasizing fairness, transparency, and accountability. State-level initiatives, such as California's AI regulation efforts, focus on specific aspects of AI deployment, including privacy and data protection.

3. Industry-Specific Guidelines

Different sectors within the legal field may require tailored guidelines to address the unique ethical considerations and challenges they face. Professional associations, such as bar associations and judicial councils, can play a vital role in developing industry-specific standards and best practices.

For example, the American Bar Association (ABA) has established guidelines for the ethical use of AI in legal practice. These guidelines address issues such as bias, transparency, and accountability, providing a framework for legal professionals to navigate the ethical complexities of AI deployment.

4. Ongoing Monitoring and Evaluation

Regulatory frameworks and guidelines must be dynamic and adaptable to keep pace with the rapid advancements in AI technology. Ongoing monitoring and evaluation are essential to ensure that regulations remain relevant and effective. Policymakers and stakeholders should establish mechanisms for continuous assessment of AI systems, incorporating feedback from legal professionals, technologists, and the public.

Regular audits, impact assessments, and public consultations can help identify emerging ethical concerns and inform updates to regulatory frameworks. By maintaining a proactive approach, regulators can ensure that AI deployment in the legal field aligns with evolving ethical standards and societal expectations.

Balancing Innovation and Ethics

The challenge of balancing innovation and ethics in the deployment of AI in law requires a nuanced approach that fosters technological advancement while safeguarding ethical principles and individual rights. This balance is essential to harness the benefits of AI while mitigating potential risks and ensuring that AI serves the broader goals of justice and fairness.

1. Encouraging Responsible Innovation

Promoting responsible innovation involves creating an environment that encourages technological advancements while emphasizing ethical considerations. Policymakers and regulators can support responsible innovation by providing clear guidelines and incentives for ethical AI development. This includes funding research on ethical AI, supporting collaborations between academia and industry, and recognizing organizations that demonstrate best practices in AI deployment.

2. Ethical AI by Design

Developing AI systems with ethical considerations in mind from the outset is crucial to ensuring that ethical principles are integrated into every stage of AI development. This approach, known as "ethical AI by design," involves incorporating fairness, transparency, accountability, and privacy into the design and implementation of AI systems.

Developers should conduct ethical impact assessments, engage with diverse stakeholders, and prioritize explainability and user control. By embedding ethical principles into the core of AI systems, developers can create tools that are not only innovative but also align with societal values and legal standards.

3. Collaboration and Multi-Disciplinary Approaches

Balancing innovation and ethics requires collaboration among various stakeholders, including legal professionals, technologists, ethicists, policymakers, and the public. Multi-disciplinary approaches can help identify and address the ethical implications of AI deployment from multiple perspectives, ensuring a comprehensive understanding of the challenges and opportunities.

Collaborative efforts can include forming ethics committees, establishing industry consortia, and fostering public-private partnerships. These initiatives can facilitate knowledge sharing, promote best practices, and develop cohesive strategies for the ethical use of AI in law.

4. Education and Training

Educating legal professionals and technologists about the ethical implications of AI is essential to fostering responsible AI deployment. Legal education programs should incorporate courses on AI, ethics, and technology, preparing future lawyers to navigate the complexities of AI in legal practice. Similarly, technology programs should include modules on legal ethics and regulatory compliance.

Continuing education and professional development programs can help practicing lawyers and technologists stay informed about evolving ethical standards and best practices. By fostering a culture of ethical awareness and responsibility, the legal profession can ensure that AI is used in ways that enhance justice and fairness.

5. Public Engagement and Transparency

Engaging the public in discussions about AI and its ethical implications is crucial to building trust and ensuring that AI deployment aligns with societal values. Public consultations, open forums, and transparent communication about the use of AI in legal processes can help address public concerns and promote informed dialogue.

Transparency about how AI systems operate, the data they use, and the outcomes they generate is essential to maintaining accountability and trust. Legal professionals and organizations should strive to provide clear and accessible information about their use of AI, ensuring that the public understands the benefits and risks associated with AI deployment.

Conclusion

The integration of AI into the legal field offers significant opportunities for enhancing efficiency, accuracy, and access to justice. However, it also raises important ethical considerations related to bias, transparency, accountability, privacy, and the impact on the legal profession. Addressing these ethical challenges requires the development of comprehensive regulatory frameworks and guidelines that promote responsible AI deployment while safeguarding ethical principles and individual rights.

Balancing innovation and ethics in the use of AI in law involves encouraging responsible innovation, developing ethical AI by design, fostering collaboration, providing education and training, and engaging the public in discussions about AI's ethical implications. By taking a proactive and multi-disciplinary approach, the legal profession can harness the benefits of AI while ensuring that its use aligns with the broader goals of justice and fairness.

As AI continues to evolve, ongoing monitoring, evaluation, and adaptation of regulatory frameworks will be essential to keep pace with technological advancements and emerging ethical challenges. Through thoughtful and balanced implementation, AI can be a powerful tool to support legal professionals, enhance the administration of justice, and contribute to a more equitable and effective legal system.

IX. AI in Legal Education and Training

Role of AI in Legal Education

Artificial Intelligence (AI) is rapidly transforming various sectors, and legal education is no exception. The role of AI in legal education encompasses several facets, including personalized learning experiences, enhanced research capabilities, and the development of new skill sets necessary for future legal professionals. AI's integration into legal education not only modernizes the learning process but also prepares students for an evolving legal landscape where technological proficiency is increasingly essential.

1. Personalized Learning

AI-powered educational tools can tailor learning experiences to individual students' needs, preferences, and progress. By analyzing data on students' performance and learning styles, AI can recommend customized study plans, resources, and feedback. This personalized approach helps students grasp complex legal concepts more effectively and at their own pace, thereby improving overall learning outcomes.

2. Enhanced Research and Analysis

Legal research, traditionally a time-consuming and labor-intensive process, can be significantly streamlined by AI. AI-driven research tools can quickly analyze vast amounts of legal data, including case law, statutes, and legal journals, to provide relevant information and insights. This capability not only saves time but also enhances the accuracy and comprehensiveness of legal research, allowing students to focus on higher-order analysis and critical thinking.

3. Interactive Learning Environments

AI facilitates the creation of interactive and immersive learning environments, such as virtual courtrooms and simulation-based training modules. These tools enable students to engage in realistic legal scenarios, practice their advocacy skills, and receive real-time feedback. By replicating real-world legal processes, AI-driven simulations help students develop practical skills and build confidence in a controlled and supportive environment.

4. Skill Development for the Future

As AI becomes more integrated into legal practice, future lawyers will need to possess a blend of legal expertise and technological proficiency. Legal education programs must evolve to include training on AI, data analytics, cybersecurity, and other relevant technologies. AI can assist in identifying emerging skills and designing curricula that address the demands of modern legal practice.

Examples of AI-Driven Educational Tools

1. RexLegal

RexLegal is an AI-powered platform designed to assist law students with legal research and case analysis. By leveraging natural language processing (NLP) and machine learning algorithms, RexLegal can analyze legal texts, extract key information, and provide summaries and insights. The platform also offers personalized study recommendations based on students' research patterns and academic performance, helping them to better understand complex legal topics.

2. LexisNexis Interactive Learning Solutions

LexisNexis has developed a range of AI-driven educational tools that enhance legal research and learning. One notable tool is LexisNexis Interactive Learning Solutions, which combines advanced legal research capabilities with interactive training modules. Students can access a vast database of legal resources, practice their research skills, and receive immediate feedback on their performance. The platform also includes simulations of legal scenarios, enabling students to apply their knowledge in practical contexts.

3. Quimbee

Quimbee is an AI-driven platform that offers a comprehensive suite of study aids for law students, including case briefs, video lessons, and practice questions. The platform uses AI to tailor study plans to individual students' needs, track their progress, and provide personalized feedback. Quimbee's interactive quizzes and practice exams help students reinforce their understanding of legal concepts and prepare for exams more effectively.

4. Coursera and edX AI-Powered Courses

Online learning platforms like Coursera and edX offer AI-powered courses in various legal and technology-related subjects. These platforms use AI to enhance the learning experience through personalized course recommendations, interactive content, and real-time feedback. Law students can access courses on topics such as AI ethics, cybersecurity law, and data privacy, gaining valuable knowledge and skills that are increasingly relevant in today's legal landscape.

5. PracticePanther

PracticePanther is a legal practice management software that includes AI-driven tools to assist law students and professionals in managing their workflow. The platform offers features such as automated document generation, task management, and time tracking. By using PracticePanther, law students can gain hands-on experience with tools commonly used in legal practice, preparing them for the technological demands of the profession.

6. CaseCrunch

CaseCrunch is an AI platform that provides legal predictions and analytics. Law students can use CaseCrunch to input hypothetical legal scenarios and receive predictions on case outcomes based on historical data. This tool helps students understand the likely outcomes of different legal strategies and enhances their ability to think critically about legal issues. CaseCrunch also offers insights into judicial behavior and legal trends, providing valuable context for students' research and analysis.

Future of Legal Training with AI

The future of legal training with AI holds great promise, as technological advancements continue to reshape the legal profession. AI's integration into legal education will likely lead to several key developments, enhancing the training and preparation of future lawyers.

1. Adaptive Learning Platforms

Future legal training will increasingly rely on adaptive learning platforms that use AI to create personalized learning experiences. These platforms will continuously assess students' progress and adapt the content and pace of instruction to meet their individual needs. By providing tailored support and resources, adaptive learning platforms can help students achieve a deeper understanding of legal concepts and develop their skills more effectively.

2. Virtual Reality (VR) and Augmented Reality (AR) Training

The use of VR and AR in legal education will become more prevalent, offering immersive and interactive training experiences. VR and AR can simulate courtrooms, legal negotiations, and other real-world scenarios, allowing students to practice their skills in a lifelike environment. AI can enhance these simulations by providing real-time feedback and adapting the scenarios based on students' actions. This approach will help students develop practical skills and build confidence in handling complex legal situations.

3. AI-Driven Legal Clinics

AI-driven legal clinics will play a significant role in future legal training, providing students with hands-on experience in real-world legal practice. These clinics will use AI tools to assist students in managing cases, conducting legal research, and drafting documents. By working on actual legal matters under the guidance of experienced practitioners, students will gain practical skills and insights into the ethical and professional aspects of legal practice.

4. Lifelong Learning and Continuous Professional Development

As the legal profession evolves, continuous learning and professional development will become increasingly important. AI will facilitate lifelong learning by offering personalized training programs that adapt to legal professionals' changing needs and interests. These programs will provide ongoing education on emerging legal issues, technological advancements, and new regulatory frameworks, ensuring that lawyers remain current and competent in their practice.

5. Interdisciplinary Education

The future of legal training will emphasize interdisciplinary education, integrating legal studies with other fields such as technology, business, and public policy. AI can support this approach by providing resources and insights from various disciplines, helping students understand the broader context of legal issues. Interdisciplinary education will prepare future lawyers to address complex, multifaceted problems and collaborate effectively with professionals from other fields.

6. Ethical and Responsible AI Training

As AI becomes more integrated into legal practice, it is essential to train future lawyers on the ethical and responsible use of AI. Legal education programs will incorporate courses on AI ethics, data privacy, and regulatory compliance, ensuring that students understand the ethical implications of AI deployment. By fostering a culture of ethical awareness and responsibility, legal training will help future lawyers navigate the challenges and opportunities of AI in law.

Conclusion

AI is poised to transform legal education and training, offering significant benefits in terms of personalized learning, enhanced research capabilities, and the development of new skills. AI-driven educational tools such as RexLegal, LexisNexis Interactive Learning Solutions, Quimbee, Coursera, edX, PracticePanther, and CaseCrunch exemplify the potential of AI to modernize legal education and prepare students for the demands of the legal profession.

The future of legal training with AI holds great promise, with developments such as adaptive learning platforms, VR and AR training, AI-driven legal clinics, lifelong learning programs, interdisciplinary education, and ethical AI training. By embracing these technological advancements, legal education programs can enhance the training and preparation of future lawyers, ensuring that they are equipped with the knowledge, skills, and ethical awareness necessary to thrive in an evolving legal landscape.

As AI continues to reshape the legal profession, it is crucial for legal education to adapt and innovate, providing students with the tools and insights they need to navigate the complexities of modern legal practice. By integrating AI into legal education, we can foster a new generation of lawyers who are not only proficient in the law but also adept at leveraging technology to enhance justice and fairness.

X. Case Studies of AI in the Legal System

Introduction

Artificial Intelligence (AI) has made significant strides in various industries, and the legal system is no exception. The adoption of AI technologies in legal processes promises to enhance efficiency, accuracy, and access to justice. However, the implementation of AI in the legal system has not been without challenges. This essay explores detailed case studies of AI applications in the legal system, highlighting their successes, failures, and the lessons learned.

Case Study 1: COMPAS – Risk Assessment in Criminal Justice

Overview

COMPAS (Correctional Offender Management Profiling for Alternative Sanctions) is an AI tool developed by Northpointe (now Equivant) used to assess the risk of recidivism among criminal defendants. The system analyzes various factors, including criminal history, personal background, and social behavior, to predict the likelihood that an offender will re-offend. Judges use these risk assessments to inform decisions about bail, sentencing, and parole.

Successes

COMPAS has been adopted by several jurisdictions in the United States to assist in judicial decision-making. The system aims to provide objective data to support decisions that were previously based on subjective judgment. By identifying high-risk offenders, COMPAS helps allocate resources more effectively and prioritize interventions for those most likely to re-offend.

Failures

As AI continues to reshape the legal profession, it is crucial for legal education to adapt and innovate, providing students with the tools and insights they need to navigate the complexities of modern legal practice. By integrating AI into legal education, we can foster a new generation of lawyers who are not only proficient in the law but also adept at leveraging technology to enhance justice and fairness.

X. Case Studies of AI in the Legal System

Introduction

Artificial Intelligence (AI) has made significant strides in various industries, and the legal system is no exception. The adoption of AI technologies in legal processes promises to enhance efficiency, accuracy, and access to justice. However, the implementation of AI in the legal system has not been without challenges. This essay explores detailed case studies of AI applications in the legal system, highlighting their successes, failures, and the lessons learned.

Case Study 1: COMPAS – Risk Assessment in Criminal Justice

Overview

COMPAS (Correctional Offender Management Profiling for Alternative Sanctions) is an AI tool developed by Northpointe (now Equivant) used to assess the risk of recidivism among criminal defendants. The system analyzes various factors, including criminal history, personal background, and social behavior, to predict the likelihood that an offender will re-offend. Judges use these risk assessments to inform decisions about bail, sentencing, and parole.

Successes

COMPAS has been adopted by several jurisdictions in the United States to assist in judicial decision-making. The system aims to provide objective data to support decisions that were previously based on subjective judgment. By identifying high-risk offenders, COMPAS helps allocate resources more effectively and prioritize interventions for those most likely to re-offend.

Failures

Despite its potential, COMPAS has faced significant criticism and controversy. A 2016 investigation by ProPublica revealed that COMPAS exhibited racial bias, disproportionately classifying African American defendants as high risk compared to their white counterparts. This finding highlighted the inherent biases in the training data and the algorithms used by COMPAS. Additionally, the lack of transparency regarding how COMPAS scores are calculated has raised concerns about accountability and fairness.

Lessons Learned

The COMPAS case underscores the importance of addressing bias in AI systems. Ensuring that training data is representative and free from historical biases is crucial. Moreover, transparency and explainability in AI algorithms are essential to maintain trust and accountability in the legal system. Ongoing monitoring and evaluation of AI tools are necessary to identify and mitigate any biases that may emerge.

Case Study 2: ROSS Intelligence – AI Legal Research

Overview

ROSS Intelligence is an AI-powered legal research tool that uses natural language processing (NLP) to understand legal queries and provide relevant case law, statutes, and legal opinions. It leverages IBM Watson's cognitive computing capabilities to analyze legal documents and deliver precise answers to legal questions.

Successes

ROSS Intelligence has been widely adopted by law firms to streamline legal research. The platform significantly reduces the time required to find relevant legal information, allowing lawyers to focus on higher-level analysis and strategy. ROSS's ability to understand natural language queries makes legal research more intuitive and accessible. Additionally, the system continuously learns from user interactions, improving its accuracy and relevance over time.

Failures

Despite its initial success, ROSS Intelligence faced challenges related to data limitations and integration with existing legal databases. Some users reported that the platform occasionally provided incomplete or outdated information, highlighting the importance of maintaining comprehensive and up-to-date legal databases. Furthermore, ROSS Intelligence had to navigate the complexities of different legal systems and jurisdictions, which posed challenges for its scalability and consistency.

Lessons Learned

The case of ROSS Intelligence emphasizes the need for robust data management and integration strategies. Ensuring that AI tools have access to comprehensive and current legal information is vital for their effectiveness. Additionally, adapting AI systems to the specific needs and nuances of different legal jurisdictions is crucial for their successful implementation.

Case Study 3: HART – Predictive Policing in the UK

Overview

HART (Harm Assessment Risk Tool) is an AI system used by the Durham Constabulary in the UK to predict the risk of individuals committing future crimes. The system analyzes historical data, including criminal records, socio-demographic information, and behavioral patterns, to classify individuals as low, medium, or high risk of offending.

Successes

HART has shown promise in accurately identifying low-risk individuals, allowing law enforcement to allocate resources more efficiently and focus on high-risk cases. The system's predictive capabilities have helped in proactive crime prevention and targeted interventions. By providing data-driven insights, HART supports more informed decision-making in law enforcement and the judicial system.

Failures

Similar to COMPAS, HART has faced criticism for potential biases in its risk assessments. Concerns have been raised about the fairness and transparency of the system, particularly regarding the factors used in its risk calculations. The use of socio-demographic data has sparked debates about the ethical implications of predictive policing and the potential for discriminatory practices.

importance of maintaining comprehensive and up-to-date legal databases. Furthermore, ROSS Intelligence had to navigate the complexities of different legal systems and jurisdictions, which posed challenges for its scalability and consistency.

Lessons Learned

The case of ROSS Intelligence emphasizes the need for robust data management and integration strategies. Ensuring that AI tools have access to comprehensive and current legal information is vital for their effectiveness. Additionally, adapting AI systems to the specific needs and nuances of different legal jurisdictions is crucial for their successful implementation.

Case Study 3: HART – Predictive Policing in the UK

Overview

HART (Harm Assessment Risk Tool) is an AI system used by the Durham Constabulary in the UK to predict the risk of individuals committing future crimes. The system analyzes historical data, including criminal records, socio-demographic information, and behavioral patterns, to classify individuals as low, medium, or high risk of offending.

Successes

HART has shown promise in accurately identifying low-risk individuals, allowing law enforcement to allocate resources more efficiently and focus on high-risk cases. The system's predictive capabilities have helped in proactive crime prevention and targeted interventions. By providing data-driven insights, HART supports more informed decision-making in law enforcement and the judicial system.

Failures

Similar to COMPAS, HART has faced criticism for potential biases in its risk assessments. Concerns have been raised about the fairness and transparency of the system, particularly regarding the factors used in its risk calculations. The use of socio-demographic data has sparked debates about the ethical implications of predictive policing and the potential for discriminatory practices.

Lessons Learned

The HART case highlights the ethical challenges of using AI in predictive policing. Ensuring fairness and avoiding discriminatory practices require careful consideration of the data and algorithms used. Transparency and accountability are essential to address public concerns and maintain trust in AI-driven policing initiatives. Engaging with communities and stakeholders is crucial to develop ethical guidelines and practices for predictive policing.

Case Study 4: Luminance – AI in Contract Analysis

Overview

Luminance is an AI-powered platform that uses machine learning to assist with contract analysis and due diligence. The system can review and analyze large volumes of legal documents, identifying key clauses, risks, and anomalies. Luminance is used by law firms and corporate legal departments to streamline the contract review process.

Successes

Luminance has been successful in enhancing the efficiency and accuracy of contract analysis. The platform significantly reduces the time required to review documents, allowing legal professionals to focus on higher-value tasks. Luminance's ability to learn from user interactions and adapt to specific legal contexts has made it a valuable tool for managing complex legal transactions.

Failures

Despite its benefits, Luminance has faced challenges related to user adoption and integration with existing legal workflows. Some legal professionals were initially hesitant to rely on AI for critical tasks, citing concerns about accuracy and reliability. Additionally, integrating Luminance with legacy systems and workflows required significant effort and investment.

Lessons Learned

The Luminance case underscores the importance of user training and engagement in the successful adoption of AI tools. Legal professionals need to be confident in the capabilities of

AI systems and understand how to use them effectively. Providing comprehensive training and support can help address concerns and promote wider adoption. Furthermore, ensuring seamless integration with existing workflows and systems is crucial for maximizing the benefits of AI tools.

Case Study 5: Smart Court System in China

Overview

China has implemented a Smart Court system that integrates AI to assist judges with case processing, evidence evaluation, and legal research. The system uses AI to analyze legal documents, identify relevant precedents, and generate draft judgments. In some regions, AI tools are also used to adjudicate minor civil disputes and traffic violations.

Successes

The Smart Court system has significantly improved judicial efficiency and reduced case backlogs. AI-driven tools streamline administrative tasks, allowing judges to focus on more complex cases. The system's ability to provide data-driven insights and recommendations has enhanced the consistency and accuracy of judicial decisions. Additionally, the use of AI in minor cases has expedited the resolution of disputes, improving access to justice.

Failures

Despite its successes, the Smart Court system has faced challenges related to transparency and public trust. Concerns have been raised about the lack of transparency in AI-driven decisions and the potential for bias. Additionally, the extensive use of AI in judicial processes has sparked debates about the erosion of human judgment and the ethical implications of automated decision-making.

Lessons Learned

The Smart Court case highlights the need for transparency and accountability in AI-driven judicial systems. Ensuring that AI tools provide explainable and transparent recommendations is essential to maintain public trust. Balancing the use of AI with human oversight is crucial to preserving the integrity of the judicial process. Engaging with legal professionals and the public to address ethical concerns and develop best practices is vital for the responsible implementation of AI in the judiciary.

Conclusion

The integration of AI into the legal system presents significant opportunities and challenges. Detailed case studies of COMPAS, ROSS Intelligence, HART, Luminance, and the Smart Court system illustrate the successes and failures of AI applications in various legal contexts. These case studies provide valuable insights into the potential benefits of AI, such as enhanced efficiency, accuracy, and access to justice, as well as the ethical and practical challenges that must be addressed.

Key lessons learned from these case studies include the importance of addressing bias, ensuring transparency and accountability, providing user training and support, and balancing AI with human oversight. By applying these lessons, the legal system can harness the power of AI to improve legal processes while safeguarding ethical principles and public trust. As AI technology continues to evolve, ongoing evaluation and adaptation will be essential to navigate the complexities and opportunities of AI in the legal system.

XI. The Future of AI and the Legal System

Predictions and Trends

1. Enhanced Legal Research and Case Management

One of the most significant trends in the future of AI within the legal system is the continued enhancement of legal research and case management. AI-driven tools will increasingly automate time-consuming tasks such as document review, legal research, and case analysis. Natural Language Processing (NLP) algorithms will become more sophisticated, allowing AI systems to understand and interpret complex legal language with greater accuracy.

These advancements will enable lawyers to access relevant legal information more efficiently, reducing the time spent on manual research and allowing them to focus on higher-order strategic tasks. Additionally, AI-driven case management systems will streamline administrative processes, helping legal professionals manage their caseloads more effectively and ensuring timely and organized case progression.

2. Predictive Analytics and Outcome Forecasting

Predictive analytics will play a crucial role in the future of AI in the legal system. AI algorithms can analyze historical case data, identify patterns, and predict the likely outcomes of current cases. This capability will assist lawyers in assessing the strengths and weaknesses of their cases, developing better-informed strategies, and advising clients on the potential risks and benefits of pursuing litigation or settlement.

Predictive analytics will also be used by judges to inform their decisions, helping to ensure consistency and fairness in judicial outcomes. By providing data-driven insights, AI can enhance the accuracy and objectivity of legal decision-making.

3. AI-Assisted Contract Analysis and Drafting

The use of AI in contract analysis and drafting will continue to grow, with AI-driven tools becoming more adept at reviewing, analyzing, and generating legal documents. These tools will help legal professionals identify key clauses, potential risks, and compliance issues within contracts, streamlining the contract review process and reducing the likelihood of errors.

AI-assisted contract drafting will enable lawyers to create standardized and customized contracts more efficiently, ensuring that all necessary terms and conditions are included and that the contracts adhere to legal and regulatory requirements. This will be particularly beneficial for businesses that handle large volumes of contracts, such as in mergers and acquisitions or real estate transactions.

4. Virtual and Augmented Reality in Legal Training

The integration of Virtual Reality (VR) and Augmented Reality (AR) in legal training will become more prevalent, offering immersive and interactive learning experiences. AI-powered VR and AR tools can simulate courtrooms, legal negotiations, and other real-world scenarios, allowing law students and professionals to practice their skills in a lifelike environment.

These technologies will enhance the training and preparation of future lawyers, helping them develop practical skills, build confidence, and gain valuable experience in handling complex legal situations.

Potential Challenges

1. Bias and Fairness

One of the primary challenges associated with the use of AI in the legal system is addressing bias and ensuring fairness. AI systems are trained on historical data, which may contain inherent biases related to race, gender, socioeconomic status, and other factors. If these biases are not adequately addressed, AI-driven legal tools can perpetuate and even exacerbate existing inequalities within the legal system.

To mitigate bias, it is essential to ensure that AI models are trained on diverse and representative data sets. Developers should implement robust bias detection and correction mechanisms and continuously monitor the performance of AI systems to identify and rectify any biases that may emerge.

2. Transparency and Accountability

The lack of transparency in AI algorithms, often referred to as the "black box" problem, poses a significant challenge in the legal system. Understanding how AI systems arrive at specific decisions or recommendations is crucial for maintaining trust and accountability. Legal professionals and judges must be able to interpret and evaluate AI-generated outputs to ensure that they align with legal principles and ethical standards.

Developers should prioritize the creation of explainable AI models that provide insights into how decisions are made. Transparent AI systems can enhance trust and ensure that AI is used responsibly within the legal profession.

3. Privacy and Data Security

The use of AI in the legal system involves the processing of vast amounts of sensitive data, including personal information about clients, defendants, and witnesses. Ensuring the privacy and security of this data is paramount. Unauthorized access, data breaches, and misuse of data can have severe consequences for individuals and organizations involved in legal proceedings.

Legal professionals and AI developers must implement robust data protection measures and comply with relevant privacy regulations. This includes secure data storage, encryption, access controls, and regular audits to ensure compliance with data protection standards.

4. Job Displacement and Skill Evolution

The automation of routine legal tasks by AI raises concerns about job displacement for paralegals, junior lawyers, and other legal professionals. As AI takes over these functions, the roles and responsibilities of legal professionals will evolve, requiring the development of new skills and competencies.

Legal education and training programs must adapt to prepare future lawyers for a landscape where technological proficiency is essential. Emphasizing the development of skills that require human judgment, empathy, and ethical reasoning will be crucial to ensuring that legal professionals continue to play a vital role in the legal system.

The Evolving Relationship Between AI and Law

1. Collaboration Between AI and Legal Professionals

The future relationship between AI and the legal profession will be characterized by collaboration rather than competition. AI will serve as a valuable tool that enhances the capabilities of legal professionals, allowing them to perform their tasks more efficiently and accurately. By automating routine tasks, AI will free up time for lawyers to focus on higher-order strategic activities, such as case analysis, negotiation, and client counseling.

Legal professionals will need to develop a deep understanding of AI technologies and their applications in the legal field. This collaboration will require continuous education and training to ensure that lawyers can effectively leverage AI tools and integrate them into their practice.

2. Ethical and Regulatory Frameworks

As AI becomes more integrated into the legal system, the development of comprehensive ethical and regulatory frameworks will be essential. These frameworks should address issues such as bias, transparency, accountability, data privacy, and the ethical implications of AI deployment. Policymakers, legal associations, and other stakeholders must collaborate to establish guidelines and standards that promote responsible AI use while safeguarding ethical principles and individual rights.

Ongoing monitoring and evaluation of AI systems will be necessary to ensure that they continue to align with ethical and legal standards. Engaging with communities and stakeholders to address concerns and develop best practices will be vital for the responsible implementation of AI in the legal system.

3. Interdisciplinary Education and Training

The future of the legal profession will require a blend of legal expertise and technological proficiency. Interdisciplinary education and training programs will play a crucial role in preparing future lawyers to navigate the complexities of AI in legal practice. Legal education programs should incorporate courses on AI, data analytics, cybersecurity, and other relevant technologies.

Continuing education and professional development programs can help practicing lawyers stay informed about evolving technologies and ethical standards. By fostering a culture of lifelong learning and interdisciplinary collaboration, the legal profession can ensure that it remains adaptive and resilient in the face of technological advancements.

Conclusion

The future of AI and the legal system holds great promise, with significant advancements in legal research, predictive analytics, contract analysis, and immersive training experiences. However, these benefits come with challenges related to bias, transparency, privacy, and job displacement. Addressing these challenges requires a collaborative approach that balances innovation with ethical considerations.

The evolving relationship between AI and the legal profession will be characterized by collaboration, with AI serving as a valuable tool that enhances the capabilities of legal professionals. Comprehensive ethical and regulatory frameworks, interdisciplinary education, and ongoing monitoring will be essential to ensure the responsible and effective integration of AI into the legal system.

By embracing these technological advancements and addressing the associated challenges, the legal profession can harness the power of AI to enhance justice, efficiency, and access to legal services, ultimately contributing to a more equitable and effective legal system.

XII. Conclusion

Summary of Key Points

The integration of Artificial Intelligence (AI) into the legal system has brought significant advancements and transformations. AI has enhanced various aspects of legal practice, including legal research, case management, contract analysis, predictive analytics, and legal education. Through case studies of AI applications such as COMPAS, ROSS

Intelligence, HART, Luminance, and the Smart Court system in China, we have seen both the potential benefits and challenges of AI deployment in the legal field.

Key points highlighted include the efficiency and accuracy improvements offered by AI, the reduction of time-consuming tasks, and the support AI provides in making data-driven decisions. However, the implementation of AI also raises critical ethical concerns, such as bias, transparency, accountability, privacy, and the potential displacement of legal jobs. Addressing these challenges requires robust regulatory frameworks, interdisciplinary education, and a balanced approach that integrates human judgment with AI capabilities.

The Impact of AI on the Legal System

AI's impact on the legal system is profound and multifaceted. One of the most notable effects is the increased efficiency in legal processes. AI-driven tools can handle large volumes of data quickly and accurately, enabling legal professionals to focus on more strategic and complex tasks. This efficiency translates to cost savings for law firms and improved access to justice for clients.

Predictive analytics powered by AI provides valuable insights into case outcomes, helping lawyers develop better-informed strategies and manage client expectations. AI's ability to automate routine tasks, such as document review and contract analysis, reduces the likelihood of human error and ensures consistency in legal work.

In legal education, AI offers personalized learning experiences, interactive training environments, and enhanced research capabilities. These advancements prepare future lawyers for a technology-driven legal landscape, equipping them with the necessary skills and knowledge to succeed.

However, the impact of AI on the legal system is not without challenges. Bias in AI algorithms can perpetuate existing inequalities, and the lack of transparency in AI decision-making can undermine trust and accountability. Ensuring data privacy and security is paramount, given the sensitive nature of legal information. Furthermore, the potential displacement of jobs due to AI automation necessitates a reevaluation of legal roles and the development of new skill sets.

Final Thoughts

The future of AI in the legal system is filled with promise, but it requires careful navigation of ethical and practical challenges. The key to successful integration lies in balancing innovation with ethical considerations, ensuring that AI enhances rather than undermines the principles of justice and fairness.

Regulatory frameworks and guidelines must evolve to address the unique challenges posed by AI, promoting transparency, accountability, and fairness. Interdisciplinary education and continuous professional development are essential to equip legal professionals with the skills needed to leverage AI effectively and responsibly.

The collaboration between AI and human judgment will define the future of the legal profession. By embracing AI as a tool to augment human capabilities, legal professionals can enhance their practice, improve access to justice, and contribute to a more efficient and equitable legal system. The lessons learned from early AI implementations provide valuable insights for future developments, guiding the responsible and ethical use of AI in law.

In conclusion, AI has the potential to revolutionize the legal system, offering significant benefits while presenting notable challenges. By addressing these challenges with thoughtful regulation, education, and collaboration, the legal profession can harness the power of AI to create a more effective and just legal system for all.